TO THE MANOR BORN

MARY LLOYD ESTRIN

TO THE MANOR BORN

With an introduction by
Robert Coles

NEW YORK GRAPHIC SOCIETY
BOSTON

LIBRARY OF CONGRESS CATALOGING IN PUBLICATION DATA

Estrin, Mary Lloyd.
    To the manor born.

    1. Photography, Documentary.   2. Lake Forest,
Ill. — Social   conditions — Pictorial   Works.   3. Estrin,
Mary Lloyd.   1. Title.
TR 820.5.E8   77'9.9'301441   79-4302
ISBN 0-8212-0746-6

New York Graphic Society books are published by Little, Brown
and Company. Published simultaneously in Canada by Little,
Brown and Company (Canada) Limited.

Printed in the United States of America.

FOREWORD

During a two-year period, I returned frequently to my hometown of Lake Forest, Illinois, to photograph people. At first I intended to take pictures only of the people, but my interest soon broadened to include the myriad objects, furnishings, and props that enrich human environments and reveal a great deal about those who inhabit them.

There have been many photographic essays on the poor but very few about those people who live at the opposite pole of wealth, power, and the success conventionally measured by these qualities. Many of the inhabitants of Lake Forest are leaders of business, civic life, and society in the large city nearby — Chicago — and, in this respect, they have counterparts in many similarly exclusive suburbs around the country. A commonality of class, education, ethnic and religious backgrounds transcends the borders of these communities. Traditionally, they are suspicious of outsiders — of publicity, of exposure. It was only because I, too, came from Lake Forest, that I was able to persuade them to let me into their homes and their lives. A certain sense of trust was established — that I would not malign or misrepresent them, particularly for political or publicity purposes. It was not my aim either to condone or condemn this society, but to try to see with as clear and penetrating an eye as possible, and to portray as honestly as possible what I saw. From here my photographic method evolved.

For the most part I photographed people I knew, at least by name. This acquaintanceship made the sessions sometimes more comfortable and sometimes more awkward, as social conventions can often curtail spontaneity or creativity. I had to work at not retreating to the role of the polite child who was inhibited in the presence of her elders. Making the most of each photographic opportunity required my shaping and directing the session to a large degree. Most of my subjects knew very little about photography or portraiture but were agreeable to carrying out various suggestions. Usually I proposed certain kinds of clothing, certain locations and props, and gradually I persuaded people into participating in these choices, if possible. I asked to see the entire house, their hobbies, their pets, and worked toward making something exciting happen — a moment, a gesture, a look — that I felt revealed something characteristic. Some people were self-conscious and resistant to this process; others just naturally were caught up in the experience.

Developing a style of photographing that seemed appropriate for the rather formal homes and life-styles of these people became important to me. I found that using a large-format, wide-angle camera,

5

natural light, and a certain direct approach most clearly revealed the structural and decorative details of the settings.

I wanted to capture something of the elegance and the extravagance, the tradition and the seclusion, even the eccentricities, of this society, especially as I became aware of the forces that are changing it. Increasing taxes, smaller families, lack of servants, a diminishing class-consciousness, all are playing their parts at "democratizing" the life-style of the wealthy. I felt a sense of loss at some, though not all, of these changes. The grand manors are impractical, and so they are disappearing; so perhaps, too, are many of the grandes dames, the grand eccentrics, and even the grand illusions.

Part of my reason for returning to my hometown to photograph was to reacquaint myself with the people and manner of life with which I had grown up. I wanted to know how those influences had affected me, and if I still felt like a member of this community. I realized that, though now I live in a style quite far removed from that of life in Lake Forest, this was nevertheless my former home and I carry with me much of its heritage. I remembered a whole cast of characters who filled my world as a child, and as an adult I found them all still there, from unusually strong, responsible leaders to astonishingly myopic socialites. I came to agree with an elderly friend from Lake Forest who told me what her father had told her: "It's not so much where you live, or what you have that counts, as what you do with what you have and what you make of your own life."

To all of the people who participated in this project, including the many who are not in this book, I am very grateful. I value their willingness and generosity in letting me into their lives. I received a great deal of support along the way from teachers, from friends, and from my husband, which helped immeasurably. I am especially appreciative to my parents who encouraged me, challenged me, but never asked me to compromise my own vision. I would like to dedicate this book, with love and affection, to my father and mother.

M.L.E.

INTRODUCTION
by Robert Coles

Not even the privileges of wealth can stay the hand of fate — the social, economic and cultural stresses that come to bear on all of us as we live out our lives. When a society is experiencing relatively swift, even abrupt changes, the exceedingly well-to-do may even be the first to feel the dislocating consequences. The poor remain all too significantly with us — struggling always, come our nation's good or bad times, for the next meal. Nor do many individuals whom our sociologists and demographic statisticians refer to as members of the "middle class" consider themselves all that affected by our country's domestic or international struggles.

In my experience, during these past two decades, it has been the rich who have, perhaps, had to accommodate themselves to some of the most singular, even dramatic changes in late twentieth-century American society. One makes such a statement not to assert a moral claim — the endurance of change as a measure of virtue, or of a class's suffering. One simply responds to the felt emotional assertions of men and women and children who, often enough, don't ask for pity, or express anger, or explode with self-justifying indignation, but rather, quietly submit — the resignation of the winner who has to take, even so, a few lumps: "We're not surprised that a few million dollars doesn't mean so much, anymore. I'm not just talking about *money*,

you understand; I'm talking about something intangible. I'm talking about the *outlook* people have. There's been a change; people don't respect a person who's worked his way up. And if your ancestors were the ones who made a lot of money, there's no respect for them either — not the way there used to be. My son came home from school — a *private* school! — and told me that everything ought to be more 'egalitarian.' I asked him where he got that word. He said from his best friend — whose father is the head of a corporation and makes a pretty good living, I'd say. I told my wife, later on, that there's no point fighting a huge tide coming your way. We're standing here near the edge of the ocean, and we can't move back, because a lot of people are pushing on us, and we have a good view, and we can swim, but the tides are getting bigger and bigger, and I'm afraid that one day we're going to get swept away by a giant swell, or be thrown back toward all the others, pushing on us."

A lawyer, a landowner, a member of a distinguished family, he stops himself and expresses dissatisfaction with his imagery. He doesn't know, really, how to put it, his sense of foreboding. Nor does he want to "overdo things." He is quite content with "things as they are." But he has noticed signs, clues — portents, perhaps. And he would be a fool to ignore them: "Taxes are getting tougher. I'm not one to spend all my time figuring out how to beat the government. I pay up — a lot, each year. You can't hand down money the way you used to be able to do. You can't accumulate money the way my ancestors could. My son would laugh at what I just said. He *has* laughed — because I've said what I think often! He says that we're doing right well, so why complain. I tell him that I'm not complaining, I'm just *saying!* But I think there comes a certain point when a lot of people who have a lot to contribute to this society are going to feel discouraged — and that won't be the best thing to happen to this country. This is a free-enterprise system, and it depends on initiative, and on a person's confidence that there is a reward for working hard and being intelligent and ingenious and stubborn. When the government takes more and more of what you earn away from you; and when the government tells you that you can hand down less and less of what you have, and what you've made, to your children and to their children; and when the government is watching your every purchase and your every decision; and when the government itself is getting bigger and bigger, and more and more in debt, and more and more a huge, impersonal bureaucracy, with red tape smothering all of us — then I'd say the future is not so promising!"

He is not so worried *personally*, as he is worried as a citizen. He respects his family, feels it stands for something: battles fought and won; business triumphs; a disaster or two somehow weathered. Of course, he has in his own fashion called attention to an aspect of change — that has touched upon the generations within his family, his particular class. His children are not revolutionaries, but they are growing up under the very changed circumstances that he takes pains to point out. Not especially interested in matters political and economic, they nevertheless have assumptions at variance with his — and not out of any self-conscious "protest" or difference of opinion: "I hear my kids talking, and I think to myself that they're losing the sense of authority my generation had. We didn't go around questioning ourselves, or wondering whether we should do something — because if we did, what would they say on the campus, or in the newspaper. We lived our lives, and we let the social critics and the professors and the political types go live theirs! It's different today; no one can escape all the judgments handed down. Everyone is more worried about what people will think. And in school there's all the talk of making everyone 'equal.'

"People are different; some are smarter and harder working, and they get ahead faster. What does it mean about a country, though, when its people begin to question themselves all the time, at every turn — its best people, the ones on top? I can't see that we do anything but destroy our nerve — make the leaders of the country feel as if they're bad people, and they should be ashamed of themselves. Where does that leave all the rest of the people? I'll tell you where: they're bad-mouthing everyone, and they have no use for anyone, and they have no one to look up to. That's what all this 'egalitarian' talk leads to — people who only know the things they don't like about others, and people who talk about their envy and their anger and their bitterness. God forbid that anyone should admit that he looks *up* to certain people — yes, I'll say it: to a *class* of people! These days people who were born to shoulder responsibilities, to *lead*, end up thinking about themselves the way their critics do. It's a vicious circle we're all caught up in."

He can't figure out precisely when and for what set of reasons this decline he speaks of began, but he is quite sure that things will get worse, rather than better. He attributes the sense of guilt, the loss of self-confidence, the vulnerability in the face of social and political attack, to the younger generation; but he himself is curiously resigned, and maybe as willing to surrender rather than fight as is the case with his children and their various friends. In a moment of introspective candor he becomes as self-critical as any of the younger generation of

his "class" — a word he does not shirk using: "There are times when I realize that the people in my class may be changing so much that we won't be recognizable. We'll all be absorbed into the great American 'middle class.' That's what everyone wants to be called, these days — a member of the middle class. I was brought up to think of myself as rich; I was brought up to think of myself as upper class. That doesn't mean I'm a snob, or I look down on people. A lot of people these days think that the only people who are 'uppity' are the 'dying rich'; I heard that phrase the other day on a talk show. Well, there are people who have no money, but lots of fight in them, and they are determined to become the bosses. They'll be different bosses than my people were. They'll be bosses working for the government, I suppose.

"I told my wife the other day that we're on the way out. She asked me what I had to drink! I said a truth serum! She laughed and asked me to go over to the bar and make her one! I told her I couldn't do that; I told her that she might find one for herself one of these days. You can't go selling the truth you discover for yourself to others, even your own wife and your kids. Anyway, later my wife brought up the subject herself; she had a whiskey sour or two and she was ready to face things. She turned to me when we were getting ready to go inside

9

and have dinner, and she said that she was sure we'd have to move out of our home one day, because there won't be a staff that will run things, and the two of us will be overwhelmed by all the rooms and all you have to do, if you're going to keep this place in first-class shape. I said I hope we can make it until we're old enough not to care. She said she was sure *we'd* make it that long, but she's known for a long time that our children probably won't be living in this house. I was shocked. I thought only *I* had that kind of thought cross my mind! And I never really believed my own worst fears until I heard my wife express them! I asked her what she thought would happen to this beautiful house we've loved so much, and to our land. She said someone would come along and buy it all for an 'investment,' something like that. Maybe they'd come and turn us into a museum; we could be surviving dinosaurs — the last of a kind, entrenched in our palace!"

He is being ironic, self-mocking, and humorous — and deadly serious. He is sadder than he is able to admit. He loves his heritage, and loves what life has given him — the memories, the daily experiences, the expectations of various good times, still to come. Maybe the dark clouds that cross his mind, his wife's, are just that — brief, passing moments that register, inevitably, a reasonable apprehension or two, but no more. In the long run, he has often said, when feeling hopeful, the rich endure, even as the poor do. (Or so his brother used to say. But the brother spends most of his time in a sailboat, always on the move, it seems, in search of a more promising sun. The brother has made his own peace with fate — has fled, in fact.) It is left for others to stand and watch and wait and live, live quite well — and figure out what the odds are, how to do the best possible. Let tomorrow bring its message, its new realities.

Meanwhile those realities, yesterday's and today's and even tomorrow's, are glimpsed in these striking photographs of a particular segment of America's wealthy people. And there are the psychological realities, too: pride and high self-regard; the sense of place, of worth — of achievements wrought within a family's given time on this earth; the various preferences, tastes, habits and hobbies — all displayed as elements in a way of life received at birth, learned as one's own during childhood, taken up consciously, actively during youth, and maybe appreciated if not defended only further along as the obligations and worries of the middle-aged, the affirmations, regrets, and high, indeed final, anxieties of the elderly. These are not, and certainly are not meant to be, patronizing, condescending, provocative or polemical portraits. These are one knowing, sharply perceiving photographer's response to what comes across as the familiar — a life not strange to her, though for some of us, in contrast, a life austerely puzzling or at a decided remove. These are moments in a specially endowed duration of time; these are, too, bits of territory in a stretch of domain that twentieth-century social cartographers have not worked at as zealously or circumspectly as has been the case with some other parts of our habitated land.

Who are these men and women and children, so readily and correctly categorized as wealthy, privileged — lucky indeed so far as money and influence go? They are, mostly, still Protestant and Anglo-Saxon — though Catholics and Jews have their own, increasing, presence among the extremely well-to-do. Certainly *these* families, shown here, are almost exclusively (one gathers) Anglo-Saxon, of Episcopalian or Presbyterian background, most likely. And most likely, as well, they are recipients of inherited wealth, quite well educated (the Ivy League is for many a third or fourth home) and connected to law, to business, to corporate boards and stockbrokerage houses, and yes, to a host of civic activities: committees meant to further the work of the Boy Scouts, the Girl Scouts; the work of symphony orchestras and opera associations; the work of libraries and hospitals and art museums and science museums and children's museums; the work of our universities; the work of all sorts of charities, appeals, funds, drives, endowments. These are families whose men work at taking care of as well as earning money, whose men advise others about what to do with money — how to raise more of it, how to spend it wisely. These are families whose children (as I well know from my own studies) go to private schools, "the best possible"; go to prestigious colleges, "the best possible"; go to dances and cotillions and coming-out parties — all of a kind that has to do with a certain "station" in life; the top of the social and economic ladder. Yes, such children experience their misgivings — the protests that young people make against parents, against life as it is. But usually those periods of annoyance, doubt, anger yield to acceptance — a willingness to pick up where others, by virtue of age, must leave off. So it is that attitudes, interests, values get handed down over the generations — along with substantive trust funds and the ability to maintain a keen eye on them.

Extraordinary havens they are — these various towns or villages or neighborhoods within a city. They are secluded and protected and brimming with the good things of life: lovely grounds, fine buildings, furniture that pleases rather cultivated individuals — who know how to dress formally, or relax with casual clothes which themselves offer a chance to demonstrate a certain loyalty to a class. That word *class* — membership in a segment of society that has certain things in common: the recognition that enables an "aristocrat," a person of wealth and social distinction, to recognize another, similarly "endowed." And if there is that kind of shared recognition, there is, maybe, another kind as well — a sense all over such communities that "times are changing," indeed; that taxes and shifts in public opinion and shifts in the way governments at all levels work, and shifts in the way schools and colleges and graduate schools view their responsibilities, and shifts in the way various agencies and boards and committees regard themselves, their appointed tasks, and not least, shifts in the very structure of our social and economic order, all combine to make it a very different scene for each one of us. Servants are not so readily available. Those who do get hired have "attitudes" that are not the old ones, the familiar ones. Aging "aristocrats" worry, sense the slow (or all too speedy) decline of an era, anticipate with sadness and regret, with nostalgic memories, the extinction of a whole way of life. The young are lured into other images, desires, pursuits — a notion of how to live that is at variance with what their parents and grandparents took for granted. "The old order dieth, giving way to the new" — but for many does so to their regret, their considerable apprehension. That is the way of history — which comes to bear even on those most secure, those most formidably endowed with life's blessings.

TO THE MANOR BORN

24

29

51

73

77

99

Edited by Robin Bledsoe

Designed by Ann Lampton Curtis

Production coordinated by Nan Jernigan

Type set by Eastern Photocomp

Printed by Thomas Todd Company

Paper supplied by S. D. Warren Paper Company

Bound by A. Horowitz and Son